To: PAPA

FROM: Steve, Jenn, &
Hayleigh

2006
X-MAS

A Day of Light and Shadows

A Day of Light and Shadows

Jonathan Schwartz

Foreword by Bob Ryan

The Lyons Press
Guilford, Connecticut
An imprint of The Globe Pequot Press

FOREWORD

There are at least two Jonathan Schwartzes. John Pizzarelli, Jr. is intimately acquainted with both of them.

"Schwartz 1" is an encyclopedic authority on music, specifically the genre known as The Great American Songbook. Schwartz 1 has enlightened and entertained New Yorkers and other fortunate Americans for more than three decades, presenting the best possible music on the air, accompanied by the most erudite, witty and passionate commentary the English language could possibly provide. And when not playing music for appreciative radio audiences, Schwartz 1 can often be heard performing in cabaret.

As a brilliant jazz guitarist and singer, John Pizzarelli, Jr.

has benefitted from the professional expertise of Schwartz i. In addition, he is a close personal friend. As such, he is intimately acquainted with "Schwartz ii". Now Schwartz's innumerable worshippers may think they understand the depths of the Schwartz ii passion for baseball and, especially, the Boston Red Sox. They will cite the many baseball-oriented programs he has submitted over the years on the National Football League's Super Bowl Sunday as evidence of his baseball interest. They may even be able to recall assorted Schwartz baseball ruminations of some sort, or they might be able to summon an example of baseball metaphor Schwartz has applied to a musical situation, and this would all lead them to think they have a proper handle on the matter. If persistent in this belief, they are all mistaken. They simply do not know what makes this unusual man tick.

John Pizzarelli knows.

"The first time I understood exactly how committed he was to the Red Sox occurred a number of years ago, when he was appearing at Michael's Pub in New York City," Pizzarelli reports. "My sister and her boyfriend had come to the show, and they wanted to meet him. This was not long after the 1986 World Series, the ball going through Bill Buckner's legs, and all that. Anyway, I brought them over. Jonathan was eating. He looked intense.

"My sister's boyfriend decided to initiate a conversation. 'That must have really been something, watching what happened in that World Series,' he said, innocently.

"Jonathan did not lift his head. He was staring straight ahead. 'You have *no* idea,' he said, as only he could. It was crushing."

The Schwartz voice is a gorgeous instrument that has served him well as both a radio personality and a skilled voice-over announcer for radio and television commercials. Combined with his extraordinary vocabulary, his flawless diction and his overall dramatic sensibility, it is a voice eminently suitable to deliver either the gladdest of tidings or the saddest of developments. In this instance, "You have *no* idea" carries the same ominous impact as does "We regret to inform you . . ." In this instance, "You have *no* idea" carries with it not the slightest hint of ambiguity. In this instance, "You have *no* idea" speaks of one thing, and one thing only— pain. Deep, lingering, intractable pain.

The Jonathan Schwartzes, both I and II, make investments. They invest in music. They invest in friendship. They invest in love. And, by God, they invest in the Boston Red Sox, a team whose tortuous 20th-century history is nothing less than Shakespearian.

On October 2, 1978, Schwartz II went to Fenway Park,

hoping. Schwartz II left Fenway Park, grieving. Schwartz I cares about his music. Schwartz II cares about his team. His music never lets him down. His team always does. But he can't help himself. He's addicted to his team.

Read his tale. See what makes Schwartz II tick. Until now, you have had *no* idea.

BOB RYAN
The Boston Globe

On Sunday, October 1, 1978, the New York Yankees and *the Boston Red Sox finished major league baseball's 162-game regular season tied for the lead of the Eastern Division of the American League with records of 99 wins and 63 losses.*

To break the tie and determine who would play the Kansas City Royals, winners of the Western Division, for the American League pennant and the right to go to the World Series, a playoff game was scheduled for the following afternoon, October 2, at Boston's Fenway Park. Where the game would be played was determined by a coin toss, which Boston won.

It was to be the second such playoff in the 77-year history of the American League. The first had taken place in 1948, also on October 2, also at Fenway, with the Red Sox losing 8-3 to the Cleveland Indians.

"A Day of Light and Shadows" was first
published in *Sports Illustrated* in February 1979.

A Day of Light and Shadows

I didn't feel much pressure the night before the game, when the manager told me that even if Guidry went only a third of an inning I'd be the next guy out there. But I felt the pressure when I actually came into the game. More pressure than I've ever felt. Even in my personal life.

GOOSE GOSSAGE

In the kitchen in upper Manhattan, Luis Tiant appeared to be in charge of the Red Sox' 162nd game of the year. Boston had widened a small lead over Toronto to five runs, and Tiant's impeccable control compelled even the restless woman roaming through the apartment to stop at the kitchen door and admire his performance, as one would admire an exquisitely bound volume of dense theological writing in another language.

In the bedroom, the Yankees had fallen well behind Cleveland and were hitting pop-ups, always a sign late in a game that things are out of hand.

The woman was restless because her quiet Sunday afternoon was being assaulted by the babble of baseball and by what she perceived as yet another increase in my furious tension. She had retreated to the living room to sit sullenly among the Sunday editions of Newsday, The Washington Post and two interim New York papers born of a strike that was now in its eighth week. She had been told that this was positively it; that there was *no* chance that the Red Sox would advance past this Sunday afternoon; that the baseball season would be over by sundown. She had been told that there would never be a repetition of my impulsive flight to Los Angeles after the Yankees' four-game Fenway Park sweep three weeks before. I had simply up and left the house during the seventh inning of the last humiliating defeat. I had taken nothing with me but a Visa card and $50. I had called home from Ontario, California, having pulled my Avis Dodge off the road leading to the desert, though I realized it was well after midnight in New York. "I am filled with regret," I said from a phone booth without a door. "Over what?" I was asked.

Her question meant this: Was I filled with regret because the Red Sox had lost four consecutive games, or was I filled with regret because I had up and left without explanation and had not bothered to call until the middle of the night—and if you want this relationship to work you're going to have to work at it?

I replied above the roar of traffic from the San Bernardino Freeway that I was regretful about leaving, and about my insensitivity and my inability to put baseball in perspective. "A trip of this kind," I said severely, "will *never* happen again."

The truth: I was regretful because the Red Sox had lost four consecutive games, had blown an enormous lead and had handed the championship of the Eastern Division of the American League to the Yankees.

Three weeks later, the phone rang for an hour after the Sunday games were over. Congratulations! From California—Palm Springs, Brentwood, San Francisco. From Stamford, Connecticut and Bridgehampton, New York. From 73rd Street and 10th Street in Manhattan. Congratulations!

Returning from oblivion, the Red Sox had tied for first place on the last day of the season, forcing a playoff game in Boston the next afternoon. Somehow this development had moved people to seek me out with warm feelings, as if my control had been as superb as Tiant's and had contributed to the unexpected Red Sox comeback. My control, of course, had vanished after Labor Day, leaving me infuriated and melancholy. And yet I accepted congratulations that Sunday afternoon as if my behavior during September had been exemplary. In fact, I had wept and raged. I had participated in two fistfights, had terminated a close friendship and had gone out in search of a neighborhood 15-year-old who had written RED SOX STINK in orange crayon on the back window of my car. I had set out after him with vicious intent, only to return home in a minute or so, mortified. The psychiatrist, whom I immediately sought out, said to me, "This is *not* what a 40-year-old should be doing with his time. *Comprenez-vous?*"

On the triumphant Sunday evening, I drank Scotch and talked long distance. I was asked, "Are you thrilled?" I was thrilled. "Can they do it?" I doubted they could. "Are you going to the game?" Well, maybe.

I had actually thought of trying to use my connections as a radio broadcaster to round up some kind of entrée to Fenway Park for the next afternoon, but the prospect of tracking down people in their homes on a Sunday night was depressing. And there would be the scramble for the air shuttle, an endless taxi ride in a Boston traffic jam, no ticket or pass left at the press window as promised, and a frantic attempt to reach Bill Crowley, the Red Sox' cantankerous P.R. man, on the phone—"Bill, the pass was supposed to have been . . . and no one's seen it and they can't . . . and is there any possibility that I could . . ."

No. I would watch at home, alone. I would have the apartment to myself all day. I would stand in the bedroom doorway and watch with the sound off to avoid Yankee announcer Phil Rizzuto's ghastly shrieking. At home, in the event of a Red Sox victory, I would be able to accept more congratulatory calls, this time for the real thing. "To me, it's the division championship that means the most," I had often said reasonably to whoever would listen. "After the division it's all dessert."

And yet. Had there been a more significant athletic event held in this country during my lifetime? The World Series, like the Super Bowl, is public theater, designed to entertain. Women and children gather around. Aren't the colors on the field pretty? Isn't that Howard Baker?

The NBA playoffs, even the Celtics' wild triumphs of the '60s, are local affairs, presented for small numbers of people in the heat of May. And what, after all, can be seriously expected of a major professional league that has a hockey team in Vancouver?

It occurred to me that perhaps one event had been as significant as the Yankee-Red Sox playoff—the Bobby Thomson game of 1951. The circumstances had been similar: a playoff involving intense rivals home-based in relative proximity; personalities that occupied the mind at four in the morning; and startling rallies through August and September, the '51 Giants having wiped away a 13-game Dodger lead and the '78 Yankees having fought from 14 back of the Red Sox. The difference in the two games seemed to be a small one: for the Dodgers and Giants it had been the third of a three-game playoff; for the Red Sox and Yankees it would be one game, sudden death.

In February, with a cable-television bill, a notice had arrived: COMING ATTRACTIONS. EXCITING BASEBALL ACTION. RED SOX BASEBALL ON CHANNEL F.

The notice had said nothing else, but it had stopped my heart. Having lived in New York and having been a Red Sox fan since childhood, I had spent hours sitting in parked automobiles on the East Side of the city where reception of WTIC in Hartford, which carries Red Sox games, was the clearest. Eventually I had obtained through a friend in Boston an unlisted air-check phone number that tied directly into WHDH broadcasts. From anywhere in the world one could hear whatever it was that WHDH—and, subsequently, WITS, with a different number—was airing at any moment of the day or night. WHDH was—just as WITS is—the Red Sox flagship station, and one had only to be prepared for an exorbitant phone bill to listen to any Boston game, or season. Between 1970 and 1977 I had spent nearly $15,000 listening to Red Sox broadcasts. In a hotel in Paris I had heard George Scott strike out in Seattle. From my father's home in London I had heard George Scott strike out in Detroit. From Palm Springs I had listened to at least 100 complete games, attaching the phone to a playback device that amplified the sound. One could actually walk around the room without holding the receiver. One could even leave the room, walk down the corridor and into a bathroom to stare glumly into one's eyes in a mirror and still pick up the faint sound of George Scott slamming into a double play in Baltimore.

The most significant athletic event in my lifetime.

$15,000 in phone bills.

Endless Red Sox thoughts on beaches, and in cabs, and while watching movies with Anthony Quinn in them.

And most of the summer of 1978 spent in a darkened kitchen with Channel F.

I got on the phone to a guy who works at ABC, the network that would televise the playoff game. Their truck was up there now, I assumed, with everyone's credentials in order. The guy at ABC owed me $150 and a copy of Frank Sinatra's rare *Close to You* album that I had lent him for taping six months before.

The guy at ABC, Sal Marchiano, was at home asleep.

"I'll try. I'll do my best," he said, "but it's slim city."

He called me at eight in the morning. A press pass would be waiting in my name at the front desk of The Ritz Carlton Hotel in Boston. "If anyone asks, you're with Channel 7 in New York," he said. "But you've got to be dignified, or I'm in the toilet."

"Have I ever *not* been dignified?" I asked.

"Yes," he said. "Yes," he repeated softly.

LOU PINIELLA: *We had dinner around eight. Me and Catfish and Thurman. After dinner, we went over to a watering hole, Daisy Buchanan's. We had a couple of drinks, and we talked about the game. I remember that we all thought it was ironic justice that these two good teams should wind up like this after 162 games. Like it was just meant to be. Some of the fans in there, they recognized us, and they ribbed us about how we were going to get beat and all.*

But, you know, we all felt pretty confident because of the
series in September when we came up to Fenway and beat
'em four straight. We all love to play at Fenway Park, and
we talked about it that night.

In the morning I got up early, around nine, and had my
usual breakfast, corned beef hash, three eggs over lightly,
an order of toast, orange juice. I like to play on a full stom-
ach. It's just the way I am.

I got to the park around noon. I felt nervous, but it's
good to feel nervous. It puts an edge on things. In the club-
house about 12 guys played cards. It kind of relaxed us. I
thought about Torrez. I never hit him too well.

I talked to Zimmer before the game. I wished him good
luck. He's a very close friend of mine. He lives in Treasure
Island, and I live in Tampa. I remember thinking during
batting practice, what a beautiful autumn day in Boston.
It was a beautiful day. You know?

"It's a game that blind people would pay to hear," Reggie
Jackson once said of the prospect of a Frank Tanana-Ron
Guidry match up.

That comment flashed through my mind while I was riding
in a taxi to Fenway Park. The season did, too. Specifics: an
extra-inning loss to Cleveland in April that concluded a Sun-

day-afternoon doubleheader at 8:46 p.m.; opening day in Chicago, and the next afternoon there; two games in Texas a few weeks later. All told, five losses that came in the closing inning. Had the Red Sox held on to but one of those games, there'd be nothing cooking at Fenway today—no tie, no playoff. The Yankees would be scattered across the country like the Montreal Expos, and the Red Sox would be in a Kansas City hotel lining up tickets for friends.

I had bought the papers at The Ritz Carlton after picking up my pass, but I hadn't read them and wouldn't now as I approached Kenmore Square. After all, who wanted to stare at Ron Guidry's stats on Storrow Drive?

I arrived on the field at 1:10, exhilarated, the papers left in the taxi, my pass in hand.

I took a look in the Red Sox dugout. At the far end, Ned Martin, the team's chief radio announcer, was fumbling with a small cassette recorder while, next to him, Manager Don Zimmer waited patiently in silence. I have known Martin for 15 years and discovered early in our relationship that he has no mechanical aptitude. The tap in a kitchen sink would break away from its stem at his touch. A zippered suitcase would open only in the hands of a hotel maintenance man. The cassette machine, though it was used daily to tape the pregame show with the manager, was apt to defy Martin at any time, before any game. I saw at once that it was defying him now, on this most crucial of crucial afternoons.

Crouching on the top step of the dugout, I stared down at the two men. Perhaps three minutes elapsed, enough time for Zimmer to take notice of me. "Who's that?" he said to Martin, who was tangled in the tape of a broken cassette.

Ned looked up. "Holy Christ," he said, aware that someone who knew him well was scrutinizing his difficulties.

"I'll deal with you later," I said to him.

"Christ," Ned repeated, an utterance that to this day remains the first word on the last pregame program that Martin, a Red Sox announcer for 18 years, would conduct on the team's radio network.

Munson was hitting. Around the batting cage were the faces of the New York press, and those of some Boston writers I had gotten to know through the years. One of the Boston writers told me that moments earlier, in the clubhouse, Carl Yastrzemski had confided that he was "damned scared." A New York broadcaster, who was there only for the pleasure of it, said to me somewhat confidentially, "This is a gala occasion."

Always, when I think of baseball games that have been played, I see them as if they had taken place in the light of day. I have spent a lot of time mentally reshuffling two-hitters and leaping catches that occurred at 10 or 11 in the evening, so that they return to me grandly in afternoon sunshine. The fact that baseball is part of my daily procedure, like getting up for work or eating lunch, inspires me to conjure up sunlight for its illumination.

Forty-five minutes before the 2:30 start, I realized as I looked around the park that in all my years of journeying to Fenway, on all the summer afternoons spent peacefully in the many corners of the stadium, I had never experienced a day of such clarity, of such gentleness. Fluffy cirrus clouds appeared to have arrived by appointment. The temperature of 68° was unaccompanied by even the slightest trace of wind, which made the day seem 10° warmer than it was. For such a majestic encounter there had been provided, despite a less-than-optimistic forecast the night before, a shimmering neutral Monday, as if God, recognizing the moment, had made some hasty last-minute adjustments. It was the afternoon of my imagination, the handpicked sunlit hours during which my perpetual baseball game had always been played.

After a while I made my way up to the press room, which is on the roof of the stadium, behind the press box and the three enclosed rows of seats that stretch down both foul lines. They had been desirable seats to me as a child, because they allowed easy access to foul balls. One had only to lurk in the doorway of one of those roof boxes and await the inevitable. Other lurkers in other doorways were the competition—kids my age, ready to spring into action.

"Here it comes!"

We were off. Under or over a green railing (now red). Across the roof to the brick wall. A slide, a leap, a grapple. A major league baseball in your pocket; if not this time, the next. You always had a shot at getting one on that roof. If I competed 50 times, and surely that is a conservative guess, I emerged from my adolescence with at least 15 souvenirs— and one chipped tooth (the railing).

Before entering the press room, I looked around for a moment. I could see myself outside doorway 25-27 wearing a Red Sox cap. Oh, how quiet it had been when I raced across the top of Fenway Park—just those other feet and the whistling wind shooing me ever so gradually through the years to this very afternoon, to this very press room that I had aspired to for so long, to the tepid piece of ham and half a ring of pineapple that I would be served, to the unexpected sight of Phil Rizzuto making his way toward my table.

"You huckleberry," he said to me with a smile. "I heard what you said."

The morning before, on my radio program in New York, I had spoken harshly of Rizzuto's announcing. "He is shrill,"

I had said, which is true. "He roots in an unfair and unacceptable way for the Yankees," which is true.

"I heard you," Rizzuto repeated, extending his hand. "You got a nice calm show. I like it," he continued, surprising me.

Rizzuto is a charmer, an attractive, graying man with the eyes of a child. One imagines that his attention span outside a baseball park is short, but one would like to be included in whatever spare moments he has available. My distaste for his broadcasts was muted at once by the warmth of his radical innocence. Getting up from my seat, I touched his cheek in friendship. I had never met Rizzuto before and had often imagined myself dressing him down before a large and approving assembly. Instead, when he departed to make his way to the radio booth, I found myself regretting the fact that I hadn't told him that I had never come upon a better or more exciting shortstop. Never.

MIKE TORREZ: *I had my usual breakfast, just tea and a piece of toast. I don't like to pitch on a full stomach.*

As I drove to the park, I thought about a couple of games during the year. After those games I had thought that I didn't want them to be the deciding thing. Like a game in Toronto that Jim Wright pitched. It was extra innings. We got a few guys on. I think with no outs. We couldn't score and we got beat. And there was a game in Cleveland when we came back with four in the ninth. Yaz hit a homer, but we blew it. You think about those things.

When I was warming up in the bullpen I felt good. I had good motion. I didn't throw hard until the last two min- utes. I looked over at Guidry and waved to him. I wished him good luck and all that. He did the same to me. And I thought about Rivers and Munson. They're the keys. And then the national anthem was played. And then we started to play. *

A photographers' box is suspended beneath the roof seats along the first-base line. One descends a metal ladder that is difficult to negotiate. One stands throughout the game, be- cause the early arrivals have captured the few folding chairs scattered around.

As Mickey Rivers, the first batter, approached the plate, I said out loud to no one, "If Torrez gets Rivers right here, the Red Sox will win." I have a tendency to think and speak such notions. "If this light turns green by the time I count three, I won't catch the flu all winter."

---

*Torrez had pitched for the Yankees in 1977, winning 14 games in the regular season and adding 2 victories in the Yankees' Series win over the Los Angeles Dodgers.

Rivers walked on four pitches and promptly stole second. "If Torrez gets out of this with only one run, the Red Sox have a shot," I said aloud.

Torrez got out of it unscored upon, striking out Munson with commanding determination. I was elated. My hands were shaking. I moved to the right corner of the box and stood by myself in a small puddle of water left over from a rainstorm the night before.

Instilled in me from childhood is an awful fear that Whitey Ford created: the fear not only of not winning, but of not even scoring, of not even stroking a modest fly ball to an outfielder. Grounders and strikeouts, and the game would be over in an hour and 40 minutes. Done and done.

Ron Guidry is a slim man with shocking velocity and a devastating slider. One does not imagine that one's team will defeat Guidry, or score on Guidry, or make even the smallest contact with Guidry's pitches.* What caught my eye in the first three innings as I hung above the field, clasping my hands together to prevent the shaking, was that the Red Sox were not futilely opposing him. The outs were long outs. The hitters were getting good wood on the ball.

---

*Guidry won 25, against only 3 losses, in 1978. His .893 winning percentage in '78 stands as the major league record for pitchers with 20 or more wins in a season.

I was astounded when Yaz connected with an inside fastball for a leadoff second-inning homer, a blast that from my vantage point looked foul. Fisk and Lynn followed with fly-ball outs, Lynn's drive propelled to deep centerfield. I reasoned that Guidry, after all, was working on only three days' rest, that he was a fragile guy, that maybe there was a shot at him. . . . Maybe there *was* a shot at him.

Torrez was getting stronger as the game moved along. When the fourth inning began, my nerves were so jumbled that I felt it impossible to continue standing in that puddle staring out at the field. I wanted to break away from it, soften its colors, lower its volume.

I climbed up the metal ladder and went into the men's room, a separate little building with one long urinal and two filthy sinks above which was written in large, well-formed blue Magic Marker letters and numbers:

FATE IS AGAINST '78.

In the press room the ABC telecast was playing to an empty house. I sat down to watch an inning or so and was joined a moment later by Ned Martin, whose partner, an amiable, childlike man named Jim Woods, was handling the fourth. Woods' usual innings were the third, fourth and seventh. Knowing of this arrangement, I had hoped for Ned's appearance. Someone so close to it all, so immersed in it all for

29

so many years, would have the answer. He would reassure me, calm me down.

"Well," I said.

"Torrez," he said.

"Do you think?"

"Can't tell."

Ned is usually more loquacious than he was that afternoon. He is as articulate and as creative a sportscaster as there is in the country. He is often poetic and moving. "The Yankee score is up," he had observed late in September from Toronto, where scores remain only momentarily on the electric board. "Soon it will be gone," he had continued in his usual quiet tone. "It will flash away like a lightning bug into the moist and chilly Canadian night."

From Chicago a number of seasons ago—I wrote it down at the time: "The dark clouds approaching from beyond leftfield look to be ambling across the sky in no apparent hurry. They know what trouble they are and are teasing the crowd with their distant growl."

We sat in silence through the rest of the inning.

"Well," I said finally, hoping for an encouraging word.

"You never know," Ned said.

I walked him back toward the radio booth. On the catwalk outside the visitors' radio booth, Buddy LeRoux, one of the

Red Sox' new owners, was in conversation with two men wearing dark suits. I heard LeRoux use the word "cautious." He, too, was wearing a suit, pin-striped and ill-fitting. It was a baggy garment that did not complement a man of position.

I studied his eyes. This same fellow, with a younger, pudgier face, had, as the Celtics' trainer, sat next to Red Auerbach throughout my adolescence, attending thoughtfully to some of the heroes of *my* youth. His face is lined now, his demeanor formal, suggesting high finance. An owner. What did he know of shaky hands and midnight calls from Ontario, Calif.? There he was in conference, having missed the fourth inning—or so I imagined. I thought: If an owner can take the fourth inning off, what is so important about it all, anyway?

I returned to the puddle for the fifth and sixth innings. The Yankees stirred around against Torrez, but didn't break through. The Red Sox sixth produced a run on a line single by Jim Rice.

It also produced the play that changed the game.

Fred Lynn came to bat with two runners on, two outs and a 2-0 Red Sox lead. It was clear that Guidry was not overpowering. With Torrez so formidable, another run might put the game away. At that moment, it seemed possible to me that the Red Sox would actually win, that the nightmare would end at last.

I paced half the length of the photographers' box. With

every pitch I moved a few feet to my right or left, winding up at the foot of the ladder for Guidry's 3-2 delivery.

RON GUIDRY: *I was a little tired and my pitches were up. I threw him a slider on the inside. He must have been guessing inside, because he was way out in front of it and pulled it.*

LOU PINIELLA: *Guidry wasn't as quick as usual. Munson told me that his breaking ball was hanging, so I played Lynn a few steps closer to the line than usual. I saw the ball leave the bat and then I lost it in the sun. I went to the place where I thought the ball would land. I didn't catch it cleanly, but kind of in the top of my glove. It would have short-hopped to the wall and stayed in play. Without any doubt two runs would have scored. But it was catchable.*

I watched the ball, trying to judge how deep it was hit. I realized it didn't quite have it, but I envisioned a double. Piniella seemed confused. I wanted the two runs. I felt 4-0 in my heart.

Piniella's catch was an indignity. He had appeared bollixed and off-balance, lurching about under the glaring sun in the rightfield corner. That Lynn had unleashed so potent a smash and would go unrewarded, that I would go unrewarded, that the game itself would remain within the Yankees' reach, struck me as an ominous signal that things would not, after all, work out in the end. The game and the season—the losses in Toronto, Butch Hobson's floating bone chips, Rick Burleson's injury just before the All-Star break, a thousand things that had created this day in the first place—all had spun through the early autumn sky with the ball that Lynn had struck, the ball that Piniella held in his bare right hand all the way in from rightfield, across the diamond, through the third-base coach's box and into the dark sanctuary of the visitors' dugout. He had caught it, he had held on to it, he held it even now, sitting there on the bench. The play could not be called back. The score still stood at 2-0.

In the top of the seventh inning I went into the solitary phone booth on the first-base side of the roof. I dialed my secret air-check number, realizing it was the first time I had ever sought it out as a local investment.

It was a Jim Woods inning, which frightened me all the more. Woods, like a child fumbling with a lie, cannot hide the truth of any Red Sox situation. One can tell immediately if Boston is in a favorable or thorny position, if the game is lost or won, or even tied.

Even with a 2-0 lead, Woods was somber. For Pittsburgh,

New York, St. Louis, Oakland and Boston, Woods had been broadcasting baseball games ever since Dwight Eisenhower's presidency. The importance of Piniella's catch had not eluded him. Then he was presented with singles by Chris Chambliss and Roy White that brought the lead run to the plate. I had dialed in for the security of the radio's familiar rhythm and was suddenly faced with potential disaster.

I hung up on Woods and ran back to the photographers' box, taking the steps of the ladder two at a time. Jim Spencer was pinch-hitting for the Yankees. I remembered a Spencer home run earlier in the year. Could it have been against the Angels? Jim Spencer, of all people. Spencer hit the ball fairly well to left, but Yaz was with it all the way.

Two outs.

Bucky Dent.

I had a fleeting thought that, through the years, Yankee shortstops had hurt the Red Sox at the plate. Inconsequential men—Fred Stanley, Gene Michael, Jim Mason—no power, .230 hitters. Shortstops.

Bucky Dent.

I leaned way over the railing, as if trying to catch a foul ball hit just below me. I was motionless, except for my shaking hands.

Dent fouled the second pitch off his shin.

Delay.

I studied Torrez. He stood behind the mound rubbing up the new ball. He did not pace, he did not turn to examine the outfield. He just rubbed up the new ball and stared in at Dent, who was bent over to the left of the plate, his shin being cared for.

> MIKE TORREZ: *I lost some of my concentration during the delay. It was about four minutes, but it felt like an hour. I had thought that they'd pinch-hit for Dent with maybe Jay Johnstone or Cliff Johnson. I felt good. I just wanted to get going. That first inning really helped. My concentration was there, especially on Munson. During the delay, I thought slider on the next pitch. But Fisk and me were working so well together, I went along with his call for a fastball. When Dent hit it, I thought we were out of the inning. I started to walk off the mound. I could see Yaz patting his glove.*

I watched, hanging over the railing. I had seen too many fly balls from the roof seats on the first-base side to be fooled now. This fly ball by a Yankee shortstop with an aching shin was clearly a home run. I had no doubt from the start.*

---

*In 4512 at-bats over an 11-season major league career, Russell Earl "Bucky" Dent hit only 40 home runs.

When the ball struck the net, Yastrzemski's whole body trembled for an instant. Then he froze, every muscle drawn tight in excruciating frustration.

I said out loud, "God, no! God, no!"

In minutes the Yankees had scored another run.

I climbed the ladder and walked slowly to the press room. I went into the lavatory; closed the door to the one stall and sat on the toilet with my head in my hands, wishing there was a lid on the seat. It was entirely quiet, as if I were alone in the stadium.

"You are emotionally penniless," a girl had shouted at me years before from behind a slammed and locked bathroom door.

That is what came into my mind in my own locked cubicle.

I also thought to leave the park, to take a walk, to just go away. Instead I decided to change locations, to venture to the far reaches of the leftfield roof, out near the wall.

A couple of kids were running mindlessly around, chasing each other as if they were on a beach. They pushed their way through clusters of writers and photographers who were all standing, because there were no seats to be had. I sat down on the roof and crossed my legs. I was no more than a foot from the lip, which was unprotected by a railing or other barrier.

The wind had picked up. Shadows dominated the field,

except in right and right center. I noticed that the clouds were just a bit thicker. A rain delay. Would the game revert to the last complete inning? A seven-hour delay and finally a decision. Red Sox win 2-0. I saw it as the only possibility. It had to rain right at this moment. Torrentially. Monumentally. Before the new Yankee pitcher could complete this last of the seventh. The new Yankee pitcher was Gossage, and Bob Bailey was preparing to pinch-hit against him.

Bob Bailey!

I bowed my head.

GOOSE GOSSAGE: *When I saw Bailey coming up, I said to myself, with all respect to Bob, "Thank you."*

Bailey looked at strike three and went away, out of my life, off the team, out of the league, out of the country, away, away.*

Reggie Jackson homered in the eighth. I affected bemusement as I watched him round the bases. I thought: Let's see, just for the fun of it, how big it's going to be. What does it matter, anyway? It's only a game.

Official bemusement on the leftfield roof.

---

*Bailey's at-bat against Gossage was the 6082nd, and last, of his major league career, which had begun in 1962. For the Sox in 1978, Bailey had 18 hits and struck out 19 times.

A leadoff double by Jerry Remy in the bottom of the eighth. How nice.

A Rice fly-ball out.

Five outs left. It's only a game.

Three consecutive singles.

The score was 5-4, Yankees' favor, with Red Sox runners on first and second. Hobson and Scott, two righthanded hitters, would now face the righthanded Gossage. My bemusement vanished. I stood.

I felt that Hobson had a real crack at it, that he is a good two-strike hitter and that he would surely be hitting with two strikes before very long. I felt that if they let Scott hit I would leap from the roof in a suicidal protest. The Boomer vs. Gossage was too pathetic for me even to contemplate.

Hobson's fly-ball out to right set up the Boomer vs. Gossage. I did not leap from the roof. I sat down and rested my chin on my knees. I believe I smiled at the Boomer. I know I said aloud, "Surprise me, baby."

The Boomer did not surprise. Gossage took only a minute or so to strike him out.*

I remained motionless as the teams changed sides and as

---

*Gossage led the American League with 27 saves in 1978. During his 22-year career he appeared in 1002 games; his 310 saves place him eighth-best all-time. Scott struck out 1418 times during his 14-year career.

they played the top of the ninth, about which I can remember little. It seems to me that Paul Blair got a hit and Dick Drago pitched. There was base running of some kind, activity around second. I know there was no scoring.

Just before the start of the last of the ninth, I imagined myself swimming in an enormous pool. I was in the desert in early summer. I thought that it was the dry heat that enabled me to move through the water so rapidly. I hardly had to move my arms or legs in order to cover the length of the pool. It was possible to swim forever.

I spotted Dwight Evans striding quickly, intensely to the plate. For whom was he hitting?

He was hitting for Frank Duffy, who had replaced Jack Brohamer, who had been hit for by Bailey. Duffy had played third in the top of the ninth, and I hadn't even noticed.

Evans was hitting for Duffy.

Why hadn't Evans come to bat instead of Bailey in the seventh?

And where was Garry Hancock? A lefthanded hitter, a slim Gary Geiger kind of guy. Where was Garry Hancock?

It looked to me as if Evans nearly got ahold of one. He missed, by God knows how small a portion of the ball, and flied routinely to left.

Gossage walked Burleson as if it had been his intention.

That would give Rice a turn at bat, providing Remy stayed out of the double play.

Remy lined a shot to right. My thought was . . . double play. Piniella catches the ball and throws to Chambliss with Burleson miles off first.

> LOU PINIELLA: *I didn't want the ball hit to right. It was a nightmare out there in the sun. I kept telling Blair in center to help me. When Remy hit it, I saw it for a second and then lost it. I knew it would bounce, so I moved back three steps to prevent it from bouncing over me to the wall. I moved to my left a piece. I decoyed Burleson. I didn't want him to know I couldn't see it. If Burleson had tried for third, he would have been out. There's no doubt about it. My throw was accurate and, for me, it had good stuff on it.*

> JERRY REMY: *I think Burleson did 100% the right thing. It would have been very close at third. He had to play it safe. I knew I had a hit, but Rick had to hold up for just a moment between first and second. So why gamble?*

I knelt on the roof. I thought, is this actually happening? First and second, one out, last of the ninth. And Rice and Yaz. Is this actually happening?

GOOSE GOSSAGE: *I tried to calm myself down by thinking of the mountains of Colorado, the mountains that I love. I thought that the worst thing that could happen to me was that I'd be in those mountains tomorrow. I had once hiked to a lake in the mountains. It was really quiet. I had pictured seats on the mountainsides. Thousands and thousands of seats looking down on a ball field next to the lake. I imagined myself pitching in front of all those people in the mountains.*

I didn't think Yastrzemski had a chance.* I thought about it being late in the day, about his being fatigued, about how he wouldn't get around on Gossage's fastball. My hopes rode with Rice.

LOU PINIELLA: *I played Rice in right center, not deep. It cut the angle of the sun. I saw the ball clean. I caught it maybe 25 feet from the fence.*

GOOSE GOSSAGE: *When I was warming up before I came in in the seventh, I imagined myself pitching to Yaz with*

---

*Yaz spent his entire 23-year, Hall of Fame career with the Red Sox. He batted .285 lifetime, with 453 home runs and 3400 hits (sixth-best all-time). During the Yaz years, the Sox made it to the World Series twice, losing in seven games in 1967 and 1975.

two outs in the ninth. The Red Sox would have a couple guys on base, and it would be Yaz and me. When it turned out that way, I thought, here it is. It was ESP. Really, I'm not kidding.

I screamed at Yaz from the leftfield roof, "Bunt, goddam it!" I even waved my arms, thinking that I might catch his eye. He'd call time out and wander out to leftfield. "What did you say?" he'd shout up at me. "Bunt!" I'd yell back. "Interesting," he'd say.

Then Yaz would lay down a beauty.

Burleson, who had taken third after Rice's fly ball, would easily score the tying run.

Carl Yastrzemski, nearly my age.

I gazed down at him through tears.

I thought: Freeze this minute. Freeze it right here. How unspeakably beautiful it is. Everyone, reach out and touch it.

December 1978

New York	0 0 0	0 0 0	4 1 0 — 5
Boston	0 1 0	0 0 1	0 2 0 — 4

Yankees 5, Red Sox 4

NEW YORK	AB	R	H	BI
Rivers cf	2	1	1	0
Blair cf	1	0	1	0
Munson c	5	0	1	1
Piniella rf	4	0	1	0
Jackson dh	4	1	1	1
Nettles 3b	4	0	0	0
Chambliss 1b	4	1	1	0
White lf	3	1	1	0
Thomasson lf	0	0	0	0
Doyle 2b	2	0	0	0
Spencer ph	1	0	0	0
Stanley 2b	1	0	0	0
Dent ss	4	1	1	3
Totals	35	5	8	5

BOSTON	AB	R	H	BI
Burleson ss	4	1	1	0
Remy 2b	4	1	2	0
Rice rf	5	0	1	1
Yastrzemski lf	5	2	2	2
Fisk c	3	0	1	0
Lynn cf	4	0	1	1
Hobson dh	4	0	1	0
Scott 1b	4	0	2	0
Brohamer 3b	1	0	0	0
Bailey ph	1	0	0	0
Duffy 3b	0	0	0	0
Evans ph	1	0	0	0
Totals	36	4	11	4

LOB—New York 6, Boston 9. 2B—Rivers, Scott, Burleson, Munson, Remy. HR—Yastrzemski (17), Dent (5), Jackson (23). SB—Rivers 2. S—Brohamer, Remy.

	IP	H	R	ER	BB	SO
Guidry (W 25-3)	6 1-3	6	2	2	1	5
Gossage	2 2-3	5	2	2	1	2
Torrez (L 16-13)	6 2-3	5	4	4	3	4
Stanley	1-3	2	1	1	0	0
Hassler	1 2-3	1	0	0	0	2
Drago	1-3	0	0	0	0	0

Stanley pitched to 1 batter in 8th. Save—Gossage (27). PB—Munson. T—2:52. A—32,925.

AFTERWORD

A Game Without a Clock

Twenty-two years later.

The woman whose Sunday I disrupted, to whom I said "I am filled with regret," is now fifty. Although we haven't see each other for years, I'm aware that she has never married. She's a publicist, living, and listed, in Los Angeles. In the middle of the night, four years ago, I dialed her number. Her husky recorded voice said: "Please leave a message. If you don't, we have ways of finding out who you are."

We.

Possibly, a truly adult man resided with the publicist, per haps a slightly older fellow, tranquil and adoring, focussed on the relevant. The publicist was, after all, a pretty swell girl, deserving of a light paternal touch. The two of them, with ways of finding out who their caller was, might easily arrive at my door, in the desert, one hundred and ten miles away. "You have caused enough damage across the board," the truly adult man would say. *"Stay out of our lives."*

* * *

Here are other things I think you should know.

Since 1978 I've been married twice, and I have one child with each woman. My wife of fifteen years, Ellie, said as recently as last night, during the Titans-Rams Super Bowl game, during the last five minutes of the fourth quarter, as she wandered through the room, and out: "I've honestly got to tell you that you're somewhere between five and ten pounds overwight, and you've *got* to exercise. You're not frumpy yet. Not *yet*, anyway."

My bad cholesterol (LDL) has been reduced to under 100 by the drug Lipitor. The doctor who prescribed Lipitor is a baseball "expert," a Yankee fan with access to "remarkably fine seats." His patients include baseball "higher-ups." Because of these "higher-ups," he attended one of the playoff games and two of the World Series games at Yankee Stadium occasioned by Bucky Dent's fly ball.

I've become friends with Tim McCarver, whom I recently told something about the Red Sox he hadn't known.

In 1972, the Red Sox lost a division race by half a game. Impossible? Consider this: the beginning of the season was delayed by a strike that was settled in mid-April with an agreement to pick up an imbalanced schedule on the 15th that could, improbably, result in an October injustice of an unequal number of games played by contending teams, a fact I kept a paranoid eye on through the season. And of course with good reason. The Red Sox and Tigers, the two top teams, concluded the year in Detroit, the Red Sox arriving in town with a half a game lead and three to play. Boston lost the first two, incurring elimination, but winning, wouldn't you know, the third game, and thus finishing second, out by a half a game.

"I'm amazed," McCarver said. And then a bit skeptically, I thought, he added: "I'll look it up."

I watched the Buckner game on the floor of my office above Carnegie Hall.*

---

*In the first two decades of the 20th century, the Boston Red Sox were the most successful club in the newly formed American League, winning six pennants and five World Championships. Since then, however, they have won only four pennants—in 1946, 1967, 1975, and 1986—and each time have lost the ensuing World Series in the seventh game.

In Game Six of the 1986 Series—the "Buckner Game"—the Sox were within one strike of at last winning the championship again. They had won three of the first five games against the New York Mets; Game Six, at New York, was tied at three after the regulation nine innings. Boston then scored two times in the top of the tenth. Red Sox reliever Calvin Schiraldi retired the first two Mets in the bottom of the tenth, but then a run scored

The three singles.

Buckner himself, who shouldn't have been on the field, was, in fact, heroic, his ankles taped and aching. He stood there at first base while two healthy and reasonably satisfactory first basemen, Don Baylor and Dave Stapleton, watched from the dugout.

Calvin Schiraldi paced around the mound, his eyes afire with fear.

The three singles.

Game Seven.

The product of Schiraldi, reliever Bob Stanley, and catcher Rich Gedman. The fault lay not with Buckner, but with Stanley and Gedman: a wild pitch/passed ball at a moment when everything else in the world ceased to be. They are forever stained and condemned, appropriately, it seems to me. If I should ever encounter one of them in a restaurant or airport, even now, with my toes dipped into a new century, I would hastily jot a note, fold it up, pass by their table or chair, and place the note before them. I would stand nearby,

---

on three Met singles. Bob Stanley replaced Schiraldi and had two strikes on Mookie Wilson before a wild pitch allowed the tying run to score. Wilson then nubbed a grounder down the first base line; first baseman Bill Buckner misplayed it—the ball rolled between his legs—and the winning run crossed the plate for the Mets. Final: Mets 6, Red Sox 5, in ten.

waiting. The note:

BOO.

Not a frivolous gesture. I would only hope for their discomfort.

Consider my own, after a rainout of Game Seven that extended the whole desperate process.*

A Monday night, a 3-0 Boston lead in the sixth, with Bruce Hurst, who had pitched a 1-0 shutout in Game One for the Red Sox. He had also gone the distance in Game Five, and now was working on three days rest. When he tired in the sixth and the Mets tied the game, I left the floor of my office, went downstairs and out to 56th and Seventh, took my car from the garage and drove through the silent streets of New York, listening to Game Seven on the radio.

The Mets broke through for three more runs in their half of the seventh. Without really understanding where I was headed, I soon discovered that I had double-parked on West 120th Street, near Columbia University, below the windows of the 6th-floor apartment I had occupied for twenty-three

---

*Two days later, in Game Seven, the Red Sox had a 3-0 lead through five-and-a-half. But the Mets scored three in the sixth to tie, then added three more in the seventh. The Sox came back with two in the top of the eighth, but the Mets answered with two in their half of the inning to make the score 8-5—which is how it ended, Boston failing to score in the ninth. The Mets thus won the Series, four games to three.

years, the apartment I had lived in with the girl who hadn't married. I had found my way home, knowing I could get in, look around the apartment, feel the rooms, the kitchen, the halls. Annie and Dick lived there now, friends who'd happily inherited the place when I left, in 1980. I hadn't been back in those six years, but here, at last, I was, double-parked, disconsolate, staring up at the bamboo shades I'd left behind.

Annie and Dick were gracious, though their two TV sets were on, their unsophisticated Met hearts at play.

I sat on the bed, went into the bathroom (the Red Sox decal was still in place above the top glass shelf in the medicine cabinet, a decal that I had applied after the last game of the 1967 regular season schedule), I looked out the kitchen window and down to the darkened courtyard, now slightly illuminated by television light on each floor. Annie and Dick muted their excitement. When tears came to my eyes, they were both comforting.

I left in the eighth, but remained in the car downstairs until the game ended.

Honking, firecrackers, music.

Everybody was up and out, joyfully hitting the streets.

With caution, I drove back to Carnegie Hall. In my office I had a drink of Scotch. The phone rang several times, but I didn't answer, though messages of condolence cut into the dark room. I turned on a light and read a bit of Raymond Chandler's *The Simple Art of Murder*. I had another drink. Eventually, I slept.

One last thing I think you should know, or at least consider.

Baseball is a game without a clock, an event as short as fifty-one minutes, or as long as eight hours. Its moments of stillness are contemplative for all who are in it, around it. It is wonderfully divided into nine episodes, with either sixteen or seventeen intervals for gossip, the purchase of meat and beer, the jostle and rumble of strangers.

The schedule itself is novelistic, each season a grand Dickensian work, with sad little moments of Didion or Cheever tucked away in the flow of events. The game is influenced by three seasons of the calendar, whose roles we have come to recognize as intrinsic and implicative. The pages of its book are published daily, the facts of its matter packaged starkly alone in a box score as essentially American as a New Hampshire primary.

That I was attracted to something as lovely when I was seven or eight was no amazing childhood epiphany. Baseball is obviously magical, a game played in the mind as much as on the field. It is an intimate puzzle, rolling around the brain in class, on a plane, in the theater, and, now and again, while making love. It will never age and never cease. The team that represents you, your choice at an early age, will, guided by your honor, remain a lifelong partner. It is you, you are it, in emotional business together. There is no other way.

So, then.

No regret.

And a hello to the unmarried.

Jonathan Schwartz
January/February 2000

About the Author

JONATHAN SCHWARTZ has hosted radio programs in New York City for more than thirty years; he is currently heard on WNYC and XM Satellite Radio. His *All in Good Time: A Memoir* will be published by Random House in March 2004.